DECADES OF THE
20TH
CENTURY

1910s

ELDORADO INK

DECADES OF THE 20TH CENTURY

1900s

1910s

1920s

1930s

1940s

1950s

1960s

1970s

1980s

1990s

DECADES OF THE
20TH CENTURY

1910s

ELDORADO INK

Published by Eldorado Ink
2099 Lost Oak Trail
Prescott, AZ 86303
www.eldoradoink.com

Copyright © 2005 Rebo International b.v., Lisse

Milan Bobek, Editor
Judith C. Callomon, Historical consultant
Samuel J. Patti, Consulting editor

Printed and bound in Slovenia

Publisher Cataloging Data
1910s / [Milan Bobek, editor].
       p. cm. -- (Decades of the 20th century)
       Includes index.
       Summary: This volume, arranged chronologically, presents key events that have shaped the decade, from significant political occurrences to details of daily life.
       ISBN 1-932904-01-8
       1. Nineteen tens   2. History, Modern--20th century--Chronology   3. History, Modern--20th century--Pictorial works
I. Bobek, Milan   II. Title: Nineteen tens   III. Series
       909.82/1--dc22

Picture research and photography by Anne Hobart Lang and Rolf Lang of AHL Archives. Additional research by Heritage Picture Collection, London.

The greatest of care has been taken in compiling this book. However, no responsibility can be accepted by the creators and publishers, or by the contributors for the accuracy of the information presented.

CONTENTS

THE WORLD AT WAR

This is the decade that literally shakes the world. The war that breaks out in 1914 is the first, but sadly not the last, incidence of global conflict that this century will endure. It will change lives and social customs forever and redraw the maps of the world. More than nine million people die and over twelve million are wounded. The Treaty of Versailles, which concludes the war, contains the seeds for conflict 20 years later. On a happier note, exploration has a good decade, with the rediscovery of Macchu Picchu and the pinning down of the South Pole.

OPPOSITE: The Palace of Peace in The Hague, Netherlands, a brainchild of Andrew Carnegie.

1910–1919

KEY EVENTS OF THE DECADE

- UNION OF SOUTH AFRICA FORMED
- REVOLUTION IN CHINA
- BALKAN WARS
- MEXICAN REVOLUTION
- THE ARMORY SHOW, NEW YORK
- WORLD WAR I
- EASTER RISING IN DUBLIN
- EINSTEIN PUBLISHES HIS THEORY OF GENERAL RELATIVITY
- DADAISM INVENTED

- FIRST BIRTH CONTROL CLINIC IN THE UNITED STATES
- REVOLUTION IN RUSSIA
- ATOM SPLIT
- WOMEN GET THE RIGHT TO VOTE IN U.K.
- LEAGUE OF NATIONS FOUNDED
- MUSSOLINI STARTS FASCIST PARTY IN ITALY
- ALCOCK AND BROWN FLY THE ATLANTIC
- AMRITSAR MASSACRE

WORLD POPULATION: 1,712 MILLION

THE THRILL OF SPEED AND SOUND

The Union of South Africa is formed and Japan annexes Korea. Black Americans unite to campaign for an end to racial segregation, while slavery is abolished in China. International police work moves into a new dimension when radio is used for the first time to capture a criminal. The Dutch government introduces state pensions. A new passionate dance, called the tango, sweeps Europe. In Italy, a group of artists produce the Futurist Manifesto, an attempt to sweep away the past and welcome speed and power.

OPPOSITE: Fire at the Great Brussels Exhibition in Belgium leaves ruin and destruction in its wake.

1910

Feb	10	First woman pilot flies solo	Aug	13	Florence Nightingale, founder of modern nursing, dies at age 91
Apr	21	U.S. novelist Mark Twain dies at 74		24	Korea is annexed by Japan
May	6	Death of King Edward VII of Britain; George V succeeds	Sep	7	Marie Curie and André Debierne isolate pure radium
	31	Union of South Africa is formed			
	31	Girl Scouts movement is established	Oct	5	Portugal becomes a republic
				30	Red Cross founder Jean-Henri Dunant dies aged 82
June	19	Father's Day is introduced in the United States by Mrs. John B. Dodd			
			Nov	20	Russian writer Leo Tolstoy dies at age 82
	25	First performance of Igor Stravinsky's ballet, *The Firebird*			
			Dec	4	Mary Baker Eddy dies at the age of 89
July	1	Union of South Africa is proclaimed a dominion of Great Britain		10	Dutch physicist Johannes Diderik van der Waals is awarded the Nobel Prize in physics
	31	Dr. Crippen, murderer, is arrested after a radio tip-off			

ABOVE: Infrared photography, developed in the United States, shows scenes taken in the full sun as moonlit snowscapes. The technique will later be adapted for night espionage.

RACE RELATIONS

In New York, African-American liberals form the National Association for the Advancement of Colored People (NAACP), with the goal of ending racial segregation and discrimination. The organization publishes a newspaper, *The Crisis*, edited by American writer and professor W.E.B. Du Bois (1868–1963), which reports on race relations around the world.

SOUTH AFRICA UNION FOUNDED

The Union of South Africa is created out of the former British colonies of Cape Colony and Natal, the former Boer states of Transvaal, and the Orange Free State. The new country joins other former British colonies as independent dominions in the Empire.

U.S. SUFFRAGE

The State of Washington gives women the right to vote.

COUNT LEO NIKOLAYEVICH TOLSTOY (1828–1910)

The great Russian writer Leo Tolstoy has died of pneumonia in a railway siding at Astapovo station, while in flight from his wife. After service in the Crimean War and a socialite life in St. Petersburg and abroad, he married in 1862 and settled in his Volga estate. While he and his wife produced 13 children, he wrote *War and Peace* (1863–69), *Anna Karenina* (1874–76) and *The Death of Ivan Ilyitch* (1886). From 1879 he espoused an extreme ascetic form of Christianity, condemned his own works as worthless, was excommunicated for his unorthodox views, and irreconcilably alienated his wife.

KOREA ANNEXED

The Japanese government formally annexes the peninsula of Korea. Japan occupied Korea during the Russo-Japanese war of 1904–1905 and has exercised increasing control ever since.

REVOLUTION IN PORTUGAL

King Manuel of Portugal is deposed in a revolution and flees on his yacht to Gibraltar. The revolution comes after a decade of revolt against the monarchy. Portugal becomes a republic and adopts a liberal constitution the following year.

FIRST WOMAN PILOT

In February, Baronne Raymonde de Laroche, a French aviator, becomes the first woman to fly solo. She is the first woman ever to be granted a pilot's license. The Baronne, born Elise Deroche, worked as a model and actress. She claims that her title is Russian.

SLAVERY ABOLISHED IN CHINA

The Chinese imperial government has abolished slavery. Until now, the Manchu ruling elite enslaved prisoners of war and their servants kept slaves. Family members, usually women, were often made to be slaves.

BLACK MIGRATION

The founding of the NAACP marks the beginning of a great migration that brings some two million black people into the northern United States.

GASES INTO LIQUIDS

Dutch physicist Professor Johannes Diderik van der Waals (1837–1923) is awarded the Nobel Prize in physics for his work on the relationship between gases and liquids. It later helps scientists turn so-called "permanent" gases into liquids.

ABOVE: The Eiffel Tower stands witness to devastating floods in Paris when the Seine bursts its banks and almost drowns the city.

FIREBIRD

The Firebird, by Russian composer Igor Stravinsky (1882–1971), is performed in Paris. Danced by the Ballets Russes, it is based on traditional Russian tales but displays strong rhythms, unusual harmonies and joy through the tone colors of individual instruments. This will mark the composer's later works.

CATCHING CRIPPEN

The first use of radio for catching criminals occurs in July when the captain of a New York-bound Atlantic liner radios Scotland Yard, in London, to say he thinks he has suspected murderer Dr. Hawley Harvey Crippen on board. Crippen, an American born in Michigan, is later tried and found guilty of poisoning his wife, and executed.

MODERN HOUSING

The modern house makes its appearance with the Steiner House in Vienna. Designed by Austrian architect Adolf Loos (1870–1933), who is influenced by American industrial buildings, the house has no ornament, the pale exterior is symmetrically arranged, and there is a flat roof. Everything is highly functional.

MARY (MORSE) BAKER EDDY (1821–1910)

The founder of Christian Science, Mary Baker Eddy, dies. Her work, *Science and Health with Key to the Scriptures* (1875), expressed her belief that disease is illusory. In 1879, with her third husband, Asa G. Eddy, she founded the Church of Christ Scientist in Boston.

FUTURIST MANIFESTO

Italian artists Umberto Boccioni and Giacomo Balla produce the Technical Manifesto of the Futurist Painters. The artists aim to celebrate speed and movement, especially of machines such as cars and airplanes. The painters develop a particular style to do this, taking up the fragmented idiom of Cubism to suggest movement through space.

ELECTRIC FOOD MIXER

The first electrically driven food mixer for domestic use is made by the Hamilton Beach Manufacturing Company of America.

ABOVE: Princess Hélène of Portugal goes hippo hunting in Portuguese West Africa.

ISOLATING RADIUM
French scientists Marie Curie and André Debierne isolate the first sample of pure radium from the uranium ore pitchblende. They do so by using an electrolytic process.

LET'S TANGO
A new dance, the tango, which originated in Argentina, has become a major dance craze in Europe and the United States. It inspires an ankle-length tango dress and tango shoe.

HALLEY'S COMET
In May, the Earth passes through the tail of Halley's Comet, which returns every 76 years. Unwarranted fear of "poisonous gases" from the tail leads to brisk sale of a so-called antidote, "Comet Pills."

LEFT: Black Hussars, the paramilitary mounted police, use mace and revolvers on strikers in Philadelphia. The strike had started with railroad workers and escalated into a general strike.

MARK TWAIN
(1835–1910)

Born Samuel Langhorne Clemens, Mark Twain, the American author of *The Adventures of Tom Sawyer* (1876) and *The Adventures of Huckleberry Finn* (1884), has died. Journalist, humorist, and lecturer, he incorporated his experiences as a Mississippi boatman, Nevada gold-digger, and foreign traveler into his writing.

ABOVE: A skeleton of steel tubing supports the tandem biplane, designed by naval lieutenant J.W. Seddon to carry six passengers.

TALKING PICTURES DEBUT
Thomas Alva Edison has combined the images of a motion picture camera with the sound of a phonograph into one machine he calls the "kinetophone."

FIRST ABSTRACT WATERCOLOR
This untitled new work by the Russian painter Wassily Kandinsky (1866–1944) signals the birth of abstract art, as it is to become known in later decades.

ROBIE HOUSE
American architect Frank Lloyd Wright (1867–1959) designs a series of houses in which long, low, horizontal lines appear to ground the buildings, making them seem at one with the earth. It is an aspect of what Wright calls "organic architecture." Inside, the houses are notable for a flowing use of space. The Robie House in Chicago is one of the finest.

STANLEY CUP
The Stanley Cup, named after governor general of Canada, Lord Stanley of Preston, is presented to the winner of the professional ice hockey playoffs. Until this year, it had been fought for by Canada's best amateur teams. Now it is the goal for the Canadian and American teams in the National Hockey League.

DEATH OF BRITISH MONARCH
Edward VII dies and is succeeded by his son, who becomes George V. Edward was a much-respected king whose love of foreign travel and public ceremony increased the popularity of the British monarchy.

POLAR TRIUMPH AND INCA CITY

Norwegian explorer Amundsen reaches the South Pole, one of the last of the great unexplored regions of the world. In the Peruvian jungle, an American explorer uncovers the remains of a great Inca city. On the political stage, revolutions break out in Mexico and China, Germany announces her intention of achieving a "place in the sun," and Italian troops invade Tripoli. The first aircraft carrier is born and the first torpedo is tested.

OPPOSITE: Captain Robert F. Scott, leader of the ill-fated expedition across the Antarctic.

1911

Jan	18	Eugene Ely lands the first airplane on a battleship
	26	First performance of Richard Strauss's opera *Der Rosenkavalier*
Feb	3	Ulrich Salchow becomes the world figure skating champion for the tenth time
Apr	23	French and Algerian troops enter Morocco
May	18	Austrian composer Gustav Mahler dies at age 50
	25	Mexican dictator Porfirio Díaz resigns
	30	First Indy 500 motor race takes place in the United States
June	9	U.S. temperance campaigner Carry Nation dies at age 65
July	2	Germans send a gunboat to Moroccan port of Agadir and it leads to an international incident
Aug	22	The painting *Mona Lisa* is stolen from the Louvre in Paris. It will be recovered in 1913
Sep	30	Italy attacks the Ottoman Empire's port of Tripoli in Libya
Oct	9	Revolution begins in China
Nov	4	"Agadir Crisis" ends in Morocco
	14	First airplane takeoff from a ship
Dec	14	Roald Amundsen's Norwegian expedition reaches the South Pole
	31	Marie Curie wins a second Nobel Prize

MEXICAN PRESIDENT RESIGNS

Porfirio Díaz (1830–1915) resigns as president of Mexico after ruling the country as dictator for almost 35 years. Although popular abroad, Díaz is hated at home for his corruption and brutality. Discontent with his rule erupted when he imprisoned his opponent on the eve of the presidential election last year. With the fall of Díaz, Mexico descends into seven years of revolution and civil war.

GERMAN PLACE IN THE SUN

German Kaiser Wilhelm II (1859–1941) states that Germany intends to achieve "a place in the sun," secured for it by its increasingly powerful navy. Germany's intention to obtain an empire alarms both Britain and France, especially after the dispatch of a German gunboat, *Panther*, to Agadir in July threatened French control over Morocco.

ITALIANS ATTACK TRIPOLI

Italian warships attack the Libyan port of Tripoli in September, after Italy declares war on the Ottoman Empire. Libya is the only part of North Africa still under Ottoman rule. By November, the Italian conquest of the country is complete.

BELOW: The unearthed palace at Knossos, Crete, the center of the ancient Minoan civilization and legendary home of the Minotaur. It is being excavated by a team led by British archaeologist Arthur Evans. These pits are storage galleries, still containing pots and jars.

REVOLUTION IN CHINA

Revolution breaks out in China against the government of the Manchu Emperor Hsuan T'ung, who abdicates the following January. China becomes a republic and elects Sun Yat-Sen (1866–1925), leader of the nationalist Kuomintang Party, as the first president.

THE BLUE RIDER

Wassily Kandinsky and Franz Marc found *Der Blaue Reiter* (the blue rider), named after one of Kandinsky's paintings. This diverse group of artists, which includes Paul Klee, value the Expressionist use of brilliant colors. There is no stylistic common denominator but the group provides a forum for the European avant-garde.

FIRST AIRCRAFT CARRIER

The first aircraft carrier comes into being when American civilian pilot Eugene B. Ely, in a Curtiss biplane, lands on a specially built platform on the quarterdeck of the battleship USS *Pennsylvania*. It uses wires attached to sandbags on the platform as an arresting gear. After lunch, he takes off again. Ely had already made the first-ever takeoff from a ship the previous year.

THE DEVIL'S DICTIONARY

An amusing and sometimes vitriolic collection of definitions and epigrams is published by American journalist Ambrose Bierce. It will prove an enduring classic of American humor.

FIRST SEAPLANE
French aviation designer Henri Fabre makes the first takeoff from water near Marseille in a plane fitted with floats.

THE EGOIST
A new literary magazine, *The Egoist*, under the editorship of American poet Ezra Pound (1885–1972), provides a home for some of the most notable writing in prose and poetry of the early twentieth century. The magazine has its origins in *The Freewoman*, an outspoken feminist journal.

SUPERCONDUCTIVITY
Dutch physicist Heike Kamerlingh Onnes (1853–1926) discovers superconductivity, the property of materials that can conduct electricity, in frozen mercury. Later, the principle is used in magnets for particle accelerators.

MAIL TAKES TO THE AIR
Airmail is first carried from London to Berkshire in England by Gustav Hamel in a Blériot airplane.

DER ROSENKAVALIER
Probably his greatest and most successful opera, *Rosenkavalier* is a triumph for German composer Richard Strauss (1864–1949) and his librettist, the poet Hugo von Hofmannsthal. Called "a comedy in music," the opera is set in eighteenth century Vienna and is full of tuneful waltzes and colorful characters.

TREEMONISHA
American ragtime composer Scott Joplin (1868–1917) puts his musical ideas into operatic form in *Treemonisha*, about a mythical black leader. Only performed once during his lifetime, Joplin considers it his most important work.

TORPEDO TEST
Italian Capitano Guidoni makes the first-ever torpedo drop when he releases a 353 pound Whitehead torpedo from a Farman biplane as a test exercise.

FIRST GASTROSCOPE
London doctor William Hill invents the gastroscope, a tube which a patient swallows, enabling a doctor to examine the interior of the stomach.

GYROCOMPASS
U.S. engineer and inventor Elmer Ambrose Sperry invents the gyrocompass, a device that is more accurate than an ordinary magnetic compass. It points to true north, as opposed to magnetic north, and is not affected by the movements of the ship in which it is installed.

ELECTRIC HEATER ON SALE
The first commercially produced electric heater is marketed in Britain by the General Electric Co.

GUSTAV MAHLER
(1860–1911)

Bohemian composer and conductor Gustav Mahler dies while conductor of the New York Philharmonic Society. His nine symphonies, the orchestral song cycles *Kindertotenlieder* (1902), and *Das Lied von der Erde* (1908), lead the way from nineteenth century romanticism to twentieth century atonality.

NICARAGUA
Unrest continues in Nicaragua. With assistance from the United States, the conservative Adolfo Díaz replaces liberal president Jose Santos Zelaya.

MOTOR SPEEDWAY
The first Indy 500 motor race takes place at the Indianapolis Motor Speedway in the United States. It holds 77,000 spectators for the inaugural event. Ray Harroun wins. He is the only one of the 40 competitors not to carry a mechanic in his car.

MASS MARCH
Between 40,000 and 60,000 women march through London in a mass demonstration demanding votes for women.

AMUNDSEN REACHES SOUTH POLE
Norwegian explorer Roald Amundsen (1872–1928) reaches the South Pole, having crossed more than 2,000 miles of snow and ice. Relying on huskies and with a well-organized and efficient team, he arrives at the Pole just over a month ahead of British explorer Sir Robert Scott. Scott, together with four other members of the team, dies on the return journey.

INCA CITY DISCOVERED
Macchu Picchu, a long-deserted Inca city, is discovered beneath jungle growth at an altitude of 8,000 feet in the Peruvian Andes by American explorer Hiram Bingham. He is an archaeologist heading an expedition from Yale University.

CARNEGIE CORPORATION FOUNDED
The Carnegie Corporation is founded to administer the fortune of Andrew Carnegie, the Scottish-born founder of Carnegie Steel. Since selling the company in 1901, Carnegie has founded many philanthropic, educational, and research institutions in Scotland and the States.

BAN ON SEAL FISHING
The North Pacific Fur Seal Convention ends with agreement by the United States, Britain, Japan, and Russia to stop fishing for seals out at sea as a conservation measure. The fur seal population has declined to about 200,000 animals.

THE TITANIC GOES DOWN

War breaks out again in the troubled region of the Balkans. Civil war threatens Ireland. A liberal revolt in Nicaragua is suppressed. The "unsinkable" *Titanic* hits an iceberg and sinks with the loss of more than 1,500 lives. Neon lights are used for advertising displays and Cellophane is produced commercially. German scientist, Alfred Wegener, suggests that continents were once one landmass that has drifted apart.

1912

Mar	1	The first parachute jump from a moving airplane
July	6	The Fifth Olympic Games open in Stockholm
	15	Yoshihito becomes the emperor of Japan
Aug	11	Sultan abdicates in Morocco
	13	French composer Jules Massenet dies at age 70
Sep	1	French troops quell uprising in Morocco
Oct	8	First Balkan War breaks out
	25	Battle of Kirk-Kilissa in the Balkan peninsula
Nov	5	Woodrow Wilson is elected president of the United States
	18	Battle of Monastir in the Balkans
Dec	18	"Piltdown Man" discovered in U.K.

ABOVE: Survivors from the sinking *Titanic* in lifeboats on their way to the *Carpathia*.

ABOVE: Survivors coming ashore in the United States.

ABOVE: The inquiry into the sinking of the *Titanic* held in the United States.
MAIN PICTURE : The building of the *Titanic* at Shorts shipyard in Belfast, Northern Ireland.

BALKAN WAR

War breaks out in the Balkans. Bulgaria, Serbia, Greece, and Montenegro unite in an effort to take possession of the remaining Turkish territory in the Balkan peninsula and invade the Ottoman province of Macedonia. Turkey has already lost Libya, Rhodes, and the Dodecanese Islands to Italy in a separate dispute. In October, at the battle of Kirk-Kilissa, the Bulgarians throw back the Turks, inflicting heavy losses. In November, Serbs fighting at Monastir, assisted by Greek forces, drive back the Turks, causing 20,000 casualties.

TITANIC DISASTER

The mighty liner SS *Titanic* strikes an iceberg during her maiden voyage and sinks. Out of 2,224 passengers, more than 1,500 lose their lives, many freezing to death in the icy water of the Atlantic. The liner, which was the most luxurious in the world, had been declared unsinkable because of watertight compartments. In the accident, these failed to prevent the disaster and lack of sufficient lifeboats exacerbated the tragedy.

MEASURING X-RAYS

Max von Laue, a German physicist, passes X-rays through a crystal and finds that this enables him to measure the wavelengths of the rays.

CIVIL WAR THREATENED IN IRELAND

In Britain, the House of Commons passes the Home Rule Bill, which promises home rule for Ireland. Unionists in the north of Ireland refuse to recognize the new parliament if it is set up and threaten civil war.

NEW U.S. PRESIDENT

Woodrow Wilson (1856–1924), governor of New Jersey, wins the nomination for the Democratic Party and is thereafter elected the 28th president. He is the first Democrat to be elected since Grover Cleveland in 1892.

MOROCCAN CRISIS ENDS

In Morocco, the sultan signs the Treaty of Fez, making Morocco a joint protectorate with France and Spain. This averts the threat of a European war over Morocco, following the arrival of the German gunboat *Panther* to the region.

UNITED STATES SUPPRESSES REVOLT IN NICARAGUA

In Nicaragua, liberals rise up against conservatism and U.S. influence under the slogan "Down with Yankee imperialism." President Díaz is forced to ask for U.S. help, which comes in the form of 2,500 U.S. marines. The rebellion is quelled within two months.

AUTOBIOGRAPHY OF AN EX-COLORED MAN

The first black barrister in Florida and consul to Venezuela and Nicaragua, James Weldon Johnson, (1871–1938) publishes *Autobiography of an Ex-Colored Man*. Johnson does more than anyone in the early twentieth century to make Americans aware of the richness of black American culture.

WALKING

Ukrainian-born American sculptor Alexander Archipenko bores holes into otherwise solid figures to convey the notion of inner space. His sculpture, *Walking*, marks the first time that holes have been made in solid sculpture in this way.

QUO VADIS

The big, silent, Italian film *Quo Vadis*, by director Enrico Guazzoni, is the longest film yet produced. It is the first of several film versions of the novel by Henryk Sienkiewicz and is an influential cinematic epic.

PILTDOWN MAN

A fossilized skull and jawbone are found in Sussex, England. The remains, nicknamed "Piltdown Man," are hailed as the missing link in human ancestry. Many years later Piltdown Man is proven to be a hoax.

PARACHUTE ESCAPE

Albert Berry, an American stuntman, makes the first parachute jump from a moving biplane over St. Louis in March. He falls some 397 feet before his parachute opens and his exploit proves that it is possible to save life in this way.

KEYSTONE KOPS

The Kops make their riotous appearance in the first of scores of films made by Mack Sennett (1880–1960), an uneducated Irish-Canadian who began as the apprentice of D.W. Griffith. His films with the Kops are made in his own studio and will be highly successful until the arrival of sound.

NAMING VITAMINS

Polish-born American biochemist Casimir Funk (1884–1967) coins the name "vitamines," later shortened to vitamins, for the substances discovered by Frederick Hopkins in 1907.

ADVERTISING LIGHTS

The first neon advertising sign, for the aperitif Cinzano, lights up in Paris. A red neon tube light was first demonstrated in Paris by French physicist Georges Claude in 1910.

ABOVE: The revived Olympic Games attract a great deal of publicity. This detail from a multilingual poster is the first attempt at international marketing.

LEFT: Five sisters working as "pit-brow" lasses in a coal mine in the north of England.

RIGHT: Still no vote, but women work the same shifts as men digging and sorting coal in mines all over Europe.

NUDE DESCENDING A STAIRCASE

This landmark painting by French artist Marcel Duchamp (1887–1968) uses the futurist technique of breaking up the image to suggest movement. It causes a scandal, but becomes one of the most influential works of modern art.

POST OFFICE SAVINGS BANK

Otto Wagner's Savings Bank in Vienna becomes famous for exposing its structure to view, even the rivets are left visible. The whole form of the building follows the structure, with much use of metal and glass. Glass bricks in the floor allow light to enter the basement.

MONTESSORI SCHOOLS

Italian educator Maria Montessori (1870–1952) founds schools in Europe and New York City following the success she achieved in the school for neglected children, which she opened in Rome during 1907. The Montessori method involves stimulating children's natural desire to learn by using toys and puzzles.

ELECTRIC COOKER

The electric stove, invented by British engineer Charles Belling, is the most successful of a number of attempts to apply electricity to the kitchen. However, the electric stoves do not have temperature controls.

ABOVE: The national Republican convention in Chicago. The election of William Howard Taft as presidential nominee forces Theodore Roosevelt to quit the party in order to oppose him.

ABOVE: Russian peasants in the Novgorod area. This decade will see a revolution in their lives.

CONTINENTS DRIFT

German scientist Alfred Wegener (1880–1930) suggests that Africa and South America were once one mass and have broken apart by a process that he calls continental drift. Because he is a meteorologist, not a geologist, geologists mock his theory.

PIERROT LUNAIRE

This work, by Austro-Hungarian composer Arnold Schoenberg (1874–1951), shocks its first audiences but will become a classic of modern music. It is a "melodrama" in which a female performer, dressed as a male pierrot figure with a whitened, masklike face, half-sings and half-speaks the words of the text. The half-singing and half-speaking technique is known in German as *Sprechstimme*. Although the form was not invented by Schoenberg, *Pierrot* shows its potential for the first time.

GITANJALI

Indian poet Rabindranath Tagore (1861–1941) translates his collection of poems, *Gitanjali*, into English, bringing this mystical Indian poet fame in the West. Irish poet W.B. Yeats writes the introduction, helping to publicize Indian poetry in the Western world for the first time.

OLYMPIC GAMES

Athletes from five continents compete at the Fifth Olympic Games, held in Stockholm, Sweden. More women participate and the photo finish and electric timing are introduced. American athlete Jim Thorpe wins two gold medals, but is stripped of them for previously having been paid to play baseball.

WOMEN'S SUFFRAGE

Arizona, Kansas, and Oregon grant women the right to vote. In Britain, suffragettes raid the House of Commons and break shop windows in a coordinated campaign of protest. More than 200 women are arrested.

JUNG AND FREUD DISAGREE

Karl Gustav Jung (1875–1961), the pioneering Swiss psychologist who became president of the International Psychoanalytic Society in 1911, publishes *Psychology of the Unconscious*. This sets out his disagreements with his colleague Sigmund Freud on the sexual origins of unconscious motivations.

COMMERCIAL CELLOPHANE

Cellophane, invented by Jacques Brandenberger, a Swiss chemist, is produced commercially in Paris for use as a wrapping material.

JOHAN AUGUST STRINDBERG (1849–1912)

August Strindberg, the controversial Swedish writer, has died. His work has been a major influence on twentieth century writing for the theater. His novel *The Red Room* (1879) introduced naturalism to Sweden. His plays and chamber plays, such as *The Father* (1887), *Miss Julie* (1888), and *The Ghost Sonata* (1907), combine naturalism and psychological analysis.

WAR CLOUDS MASS IN THE BALKANS

Trouble continues in the Balkans as the world drifts towards war. Revolution intensifies in Mexico, where the first air-to-air combat takes place. Stravinsky's *Rite of Spring* causes a riot, and in New York, the Armory Show gives Americans their first chance to view examples of European modern art. Also in New York, the new Woolworth Building is the world's tallest. Vitamins A and B are isolated and state-funded insurance is introduced into Britain.

1913

Feb	2	Grand Central Station, the world's largest train station, opens in New York
	23	Deposed Mexican President Madero is shot
Mar	18	King George I of Greece is assassinated in Salonika
May	10	Bombs are dropped on Mexican gunboats
	29	Igor Stravinsky's ballet, *The Rite of Spring, is* performed in Paris to riots
	30	Treaty ends the First Balkan War
June	8	British suffragette Emily Davison is killed by a horse
June	30	Second Balkan War breaks out as Bulgaria attacks Serbia
Aug	10	Treaty of Bucharest ends the Second Balkan War
Sep	29	Rudolf Diesel, inventor of the diesel engine, dies at age 55
Oct	10	Last rock barrier on the Panama Canal is blasted away by President Wilson
Dec	10	Indian Poet Rabindranath Tagore is awarded the Nobel Prize in literature

OPPOSITE: British suffragette Emily Davison lies fatally injured after falling under the king's horse, Anmer, during the annual Derby race.

ABOVE: One of Eadweard Muybridge's remarkable photographs capturing the body in movement. Muybridge's work has great influence on artists of the day.

BALKAN WARS

In March, Adrianople surrenders to the Bulgarians, who have been besieging the city, and in May a peace treaty is signed with the Turks. However, war breaks out again and the Turks reoccupy Adrianople. After bitter fighting, in August peace is finally restored to the Balkans after a year of war. The treaty limits the Ottoman Empire in Europe to Constantinople and its neighbors, creates the new state of Albania, doubles the size of Serbia and Montenegro, and confirms Greece as the most important power in the Aegean Sea. Both Bulgaria and Turkey bitterly resent the new settlement.

MEXICAN REVOLUTION

Right wing general Victoriano Huerta seizes power from elected president Madero, who is murdered. Huerta's dictatorial regime leads to revolts led by General Alvaro Obregon and revolutionaries Francisco "Pancho" Villa and Emiliano Zapata. In May, pilot Didier Masson, a supporter of the rebels, drops the first-ever bombs on an enemy warship when he attacks Mexican gunships in Guayamas Bay. In November, the first air-to-air combat takes place when an aircraft piloted by Phillip Rader, in support of President Huerta, exchanges pistol shots with a rebel plane flown by Dean Ivan Lamb.

A BOY'S WILL

American poet Robert Frost (1874–1963) publishes his first volume of poetry and an authentically American voice is heard in modern poetry.

PANAMA CANAL OPENS

The canal connecting the Pacific and Atlantic oceans is finally opened. Only small vessels can travel through at this time, but larger ships will be able to pass through the canal sometime next year.

GREEK KING ASSASSINATED

King George I of Greece is assassinated by a madman, Alexander Schinas, in Salonika, newly won from the Ottoman Turks. George had been king since 1863. He is succeeded by his son, Constantine I.

WOMEN'S SUFFRAGE

In the United States, Alice Paul and Lucy Burns lead a parade of 5,000 through Washington, D.C. demanding women's suffrage on the day before President Wilson's inauguration. In the U.K., British suffragette Emily Davison dies after falling under the hooves of the king's horse in the Derby.

LES GRANDES MEAULNES

In his one completed novel, *Les Grandes Meaulnes*, French writer Alain-Fournier (1886–1914), who will die in the first weeks of World War I, evokes a dream world and a world of childhood, both of which are finally lost. It is one of the few successful novels to come from the symbolist movement in art and literature.

THE FOURTH OF JULY

In this new work, American composer Charles Ives (1874–1954) creates a unique sound world, full of snatches of American tunes. Its technique and harmonies anticipate many later developments. Ives is an insurance executive who composes in his free time.

SPRING RITE CAUSES RIOTS

The *Rite of Spring*, a new work by Russian composer Igor Stravinsky (1882–1971), is premiered in Paris. Staged by the Ballets Russes, it portrays a fertility rite that ends in a ritual sacrifice, and it causes a riot in the theater. With its strong rhythms and vibrant orchestral colors, the work will later become one of the most popular in twentieth century music.

SWANN'S WAY

The first part of French writer Marcel Proust's great novel, *A la Recherche du Temps Perdu* (1913–1927), is published. Its evocation of memory and character over a large canvas make it one of the most important of literary works. Proust's literary goal is to release creative energies derived from past experience, from the hidden store of the unconscious.

ISOTOPES

British chemist Frederick Soddy (1877–1956) invents the term "isotope" to describe atoms of the same element that have different masses. For example, carbon-12, the most common form of that element, has a different mass than carbon-14, which is radioactive.

ARMORY SHOW

Some 1,600 works are exhibited at the Armory Show in New York City, including around 400 modern European works. This gives Americans the chance to see many European modern works for the first time and gives modern artists much publicity. Some of the paintings, such as Matisse's *Blue Nude* (which was burned in effigy) and Duchamp's *Nude Descending a Staircase*, cause controversy.

WORLD'S TALLEST BUILDING

The Woolworth Building in New York City, architect Cass Gilbert's Gothic-style skyscraper, is 790 feet high. It is the tallest building in the world. It is so high that it influences the decision to introduce zoning, whereby tall buildings have to be set back to provide light and improve wind flow.

SOCIOLOGY PROFESSOR

Pioneering French sociologist Emile Durkheim (1858–1917) becomes the first professor of sociology at the Sorbonne, Paris. In *The Rules of Sociological Method* (1895), he advocates using the scientific method to study society. He believes that studying anthropology will throw light on the way society is organized.

PRIZE FOR ONNES

The Dutch scientist Heike Kamelingh Onnes is awarded the Nobel Prize in physics for liquifying helium.

BELOW: Members of the Scott expedition to the Antarctic, including Captain Scott (center) and Captain Oates (second from the right). Five of the group died, including Scott himself.

STAINLESS STEEL

Metallurgists Henry Brearley (U.K.) and F.M. Becket (U.S.A.) produce stainless steel, an alloy of iron and chromium which resists rust.

GAS-FILLED BULBS

American chemist Irving Langmuir discovers that electric light bulbs last longer if they are filled with an inert gas such as nitrogen or argon.

NATIONAL INSURANCE

In Britain, payments are to be made to British workers under a new National Health Insurance Act. Under this, state and employers will give limited financial support during ill-health and unemployment. The state insurance scheme is based on pioneering schemes set up by Scandinavian governments in the late nineteenth century and the Dutch government in 1901.

OZONE LAYER FOUND

French physicist Charles Fabry discovers that there are quantities of ozone in the upper atmosphere, between 6 and 26 miles above the Earth.

SCHWEITZER'S HOSPITAL

Albert Schweitzer's new hospital is opened in Lambarene, French Equatorial Africa. It will treat thousands of people suffering from tropical diseases.

VITAMINS A AND B

American biochemist Elmer Verner McCollum discovers fat-soluble vitamins A and B.

DEN NORWEGERN

BEHAVIORISM

In *Behaviorism*, John Broadus Watson (1878–1958), an American psychology professor, argues that psychology is the study of observable behavior, which is a response to physiological stimulus. His approach to psychology is well received by psychologists who question the value of studying the unconscious.

ARTIFICIAL KIDNEY

Medical theories come close to reality when American pharmacologist John James Abel and his colleagues make the first artificial kidney. However, it is not completely practicable.

LEFT: An impressive present from the German Kaiser to the people of Norway, the colossal statue of Frijthof.

BELOW: Diamond hunters race to peg their claim at Killarney, dubbed the new "Eldorado" of South Africa.

DOMESTIC FRIDGE ON SALE

The first domestic electric refrigerator goes on sale in Chicago. Called the Domelre, its compressor (which compresses air to reduce the temperature) is driven by an electric motor instead of the steam engine used on earlier refrigerators.

HARRIET TUBMAN
(1821–1913)

Former American slave, Harriet Tubman, has died at her home in Auburn, New York. A courageous woman, known as the "Moses of her people," she smuggled more than 300 slaves to freedom via the so-called Underground Railroad after her own escape from slavery.

THE END OF THE GOLDEN SUMMER

Archduke Ferdinand is assassinated in Sarajevo. The rival European powers mobilize and by August, France, Britain, and Russia are at war with Germany and Austria-Hungary. The world's first global conflict is under way. Elsewhere, the Panama Canal opens and Mother's Day is invented.

OPPOSITE: Soldiers struggle to maneuver in the muddy trenches characteristic of World War I.

1914

June	28	Serbian student Gavrilo Princip assassinates Archduke Franz Ferdinand of Austria in Sarajevo
July	28	Austria-Hungary declares war on Serbia
	29	Russia mobilizes its army
	30	In Britain, the Irish Home Rule Bill is shelved
Aug	1	Germany declares war on Russia because of Russian mobilization
	3	Germany declares war on Russia's ally, France
	4	Germany invades Belgium in order to reach France, Britain then declares war on Germany
	5	First traffic lights are introduced in the United States
	6	Austria-Hungary declares war on Russia
	15	Official opening of the Panama Canal
	23	Battle of Mons: British army sent to help Belgium, but begins to retreat

Aug	26	Battle of Tannenberg begins. It is a huge German victory against Russia
Sep	5	Germans capture Reims, France
	6–8	Battle of the Marne: German advance halted
	19	South African troops invade German West Africa (Namibia)
	22	Germans sink British cruisers off the Netherlands
Oct	29	The Ottoman Empire (Turkey) joins the war on Germany's side
	30	Battle of Ypres begins
Nov	11	Trench warfare fully established on the Western Front in France
Dec	11	Battle of the Falklands: four German cruisers sunk
	25	Christmas Day truce on the Western Front: German and Allied troops play soccer

WORLD WAR I BREAKS OUT

In Sarajevo, Bosnia, Archduke Franz Ferdinand, heir to the Austrian throne, is assassinated by a Serb, Gavrilo Princip, in June. The Austrian government suspects Serbia of complicity in the killing and threatens reprisals. As a result of the assassination in Sarajevo, the rival European powers mobilize their armies. Austria declares war on Serbia, which is supported by Russia, and invades. Germany declares its support for Austria and declares war on Russia. France supports Russia and prepares for war. In August, Germany invades Belgium on its way to invade France. As a result, Britain declares war on Germany to protect Belgian neutrality. Italy, the Netherlands, Spain, Portugal, and the Scandinavian countries stay out of the war, which engulfs the whole of the rest of Europe. In September, the war spreads to the Pacific and Africa as British and Empire troops invade and seize the German colonies of Togo, Cameroon, German East Africa, German Southwest Africa, New Guinea, and the Caroline Islands. Fighting is now taking place around the world.

BELOW: Aircraft soon join the conflict on both sides.

ABOVE: HMS *Iron Duke* battles through the North Sea.

ABOVE: Dropping bombs from an airplane.

ABOVE: American artillery plays a crucial role in the final year of the war. This is a 16 inch pack gun that can be mounted on a railroad carriage for ease of maneuvering and firing.

ABOVE: German submarine crew in the North Sea.

LEFT: German high command plan tactics and strategy in the field.

RIGHT: Going over the top. As soldiers emerged from the trenches, they were only too often mown down.

OPPOSITE BELOW: Austrian troops shoot blindfolded prisoners.

FIRST SCREEN GODDESS
American actress Mary Pickford (1893–1979) stars in Edward S. Porter's film, *Tess of the Storm Country*. This is her first famous movie, and one of the hits that launches her as the "first screen goddess."

FIRST TARZAN
Written by Edgar Rice Burroughs, *Tarzan of the Apes* is published. It is the first of a series of books featuring Tarzan, a British aristocrat who is abandoned in the jungle and brought up by apes.

PANAMA CANAL OPENS
The Panama Canal is officially opened to traffic in August, having taken ten years to build at a cost of $380 million. It shortens a voyage from New York to San Francisco by about 7,750 miles.

A PORTRAIT OF THE ARTIST AS A YOUNG MAN
The seminal autobiographical novel, *A Portrait of the Artist as a Young Man*, by Irish writer James Joyce (1882–1941), begins serial publication in *The Egoist*. It is the archetypal *Bildungsroman* and inspires other writers. *Dubliners*, Joyce's volume of short stories, also appears this year.

FIRST TRAFFIC LIGHTS
As motor vehicles increase in number, the first two-color electric traffic lights, red and green, are installed in Cleveland, Ohio, at the junction of Euclid Avenue and 105th Street.

SUFFRAGETTES SIGN FOR WAR
After fighting the British government for many years, suffragettes Emmeline and Christabel Pankhurst urge women to join the war effort. Many respond to the call; some join an international women's peace movement.

HORMONE ISOLATED
American biochemist Edward Calvin Kendall (1886–1972) isolates the hormone thyroxin, in crystalline form. This hormone is essential for physical growth and mental development.

A BLUE NOTE
Black composer W.C. Handy (1873–1958) becomes known as "the father of the blues" with numbers such as *St Louis Blues*. He integrates ragtime and jazz styles and produces a characteristic effect with a "blue note," a slightly flattened seventh note of the scale, which comes from traditional black music.

MOTHER'S DAY
Mother's Day is introduced in the United States. This follows lobbying by Anna Jarvis of West Virginia, who marks May 10, the day her mother died, with prayers. Congress signs a resolution that the second Sunday in May is to be a national holiday.

EARTH'S CORE
By studying earthquake waves, American geologist Beno Gutenberg decides that the Earth has a central core, a theory now generally accepted.

EARLY BRASSIERE
The first brassiere is marketed, based on a design by Mary Phelps Jacob, a New York socialite. Her first model is made from two handkerchiefs and some elastic.

SOCCER IN THE TRENCHES
During a Christmas Day truce, German and British soldiers fighting in France play soccer together in the no-man's land between their trenches. The following day, they return to killing one other.

GAS, GALLIPOLI, AND ZEPPELIN RAIDS

Far from ending by Christmas, the Great War intensifies. Improved technology makes the machine gun a terrible weapon of war and both sides make use of poison gas, with awful results. Zeppelins bomb British cities. Italy enters the war. The *Lusitania* is sunk by a German submarine. While men make war, some women travel to The Hague to discuss possible ways of achieving peace. Radio waves are sent across the Atlantic. In the United States, the white racist organization the Ku Klux Klan is revived.

OPPOSITE: Turkish troops at Gallipoli, the campaign that lasted for almost a year.

1915

Jan	9	German zeppelins bomb English towns	**Aug**	6	Warsaw falls to German troops
				30	Germans capture the Russian fortress of Brest-Litovsk
Feb	2	Germany begins U-boat blockade of the British Isles	**Sep**	8	Czar Nicholas II takes command of the Russian army away from Grand Duke Nicholas
	19	British ships shell Turkish forts guarding the Dardanelles Strait			
Apr	22	First use of poison gas by Germans at Ypres	**Oct**	7	French and British troops land at Salonika, Greece
	25	British, Australian, and New Zealand troops land at Gallipoli, in the Dardanelles		12	British nurse Edith Cavell is shot in German-occupied Belgium
			Nov	5	An airplane is catapulted from a U.S. warship, the first such launch
May	7	German U-boat sinks the British liner *Lusitania*			
	23	Italy declares war on Austria-Hungary	**Dec**	10	The 100th car rolls off the Ford assembly line
				20	The Gallipoli campaign is abandoned
June	1	Zeppelins bomb London			

ITALY ENTERS THE WAR

After renouncing the Triple Alliance with Germany and Austria, Italy enters the war and seizes Italian-speaking territory from Austria. Despite its early successes, the Italian army fights a series of inconclusive battles on the River Isonzo against the Austrians.

HOLLAND REMAINS NEUTRAL

Holland maintained neutrality during the course of World War I.

SINKING OF THE LUSITANIA

The liner *Lusitania* sinks off the coast of Ireland after it is torpedoed without warning by a German submarine. More than 1,100 of the 1,978 on board are drowned, including 128 American citizens. The sinking increases anti-German sentiment in the United States, which is trying to remain neutral in the war.

NURSE SHOT

In Belgium, the British nurse Edith Cavell (b. 1865) is shot by a German firing squad for sheltering Belgians fearful of conscription and helping young British and French soldiers escape to safety across the Dutch border. Her death causes an international outrage against the German action.

SYNCHRONIZED MACHINE GUN

Germany introduces a device that synchronizes a machine gun so that its bullets can be fired through an aircraft's rotating propeller without hitting the blades. The gun is fitted into a Fokker E-1 fighter plane.

POISON GAS

German armies use chlorine gas for the first time against the British at Ypres. Its effects are devastating and over the next four years, both sides develop phosgene and mustard gas, causing terrible injuries and deaths. English physicist Hertha Ayrton (1854–1923) works on a fan for dispersing gas. It is later known as the Ayrton fan.

WOMEN AT THE HAGUE

In April, 2,000 women delegates from many countries meet at The Hague in Holland to discuss ways of ending the war. They set up the Women's International League for Peace and Freedom (WILPF) and agree to lobby governments for peace. By November, women have formed peace groups in 11 European countries including Austria, Belgium, Britain, Germany, Italy, France, and Hungary.

ABOVE: The ominous Ku Klux Klan regroups in Atlanta, Georgia.

LEFT: The passenger ship *Lusitania*, soon to be a victim of war.

KKK REVIVED
The Ku Klux Klan white supremacist movement, which arose after the Civil War in the American South, is revived in Atlanta by ex-preacher William J. Simmons.

THE GOOD SOLDIER
The publication of *The Good Soldier* by English novelist Ford Madox Ford (1873–1939) brings him fame. The novel is valued for its subtle treatment of life's illusions and realities. Ford is also known for his championing of experiment in fiction and his support for important writers, such as D.H. Lawrence, at early stages in their careers.

HIGHER EDUCATION FOR CHINESE WOMEN
Ginling College, the first institution of higher education for women, opens in Nanking, China.

THE BIRTH OF A NATION
The most famous of American film director D.W. Griffith's great silent epics, *The Birth of a Nation*, is screened this year. It covers the Civil War and is remarkable for its use of such cinematic techniques as close-ups, fade-outs, and flashbacks. But Griffith (1875–1948) is criticized for the film's racial bias and glorification of the Ku Klux Klan.

HERLAND
Having written a famous short story, *The Yellow Wallpaper* (1892), about a young Victorian woman's mental breakdown, American feminist Charlotte Perkins Gilman (1860–1935) publishes *Herland*, a feminist utopia.

CALLING LONG DISTANCE
In January, the first North American transcontinental telephone service between New York City and San Francisco is opened by the inventor of the telephone, the Scotsman Alexander Graham Bell (1847–1922), and his former assistant Thomas Watson.

BELOW: German submarine in rough seas.

ABOVE: Sinking of the German cruiser *Bluecher* in the North Sea.

ABOVE: A Turkish field hospital at Gallipoli.

CATAPULTED INTO THE AIR

In November, a flying boat is catapulted from the deck of the U.S. battleship *Carolina* in Pensacola Bay, Fl. It is the first aircraft launched at sea in this manner.

BLACK SQUARE

Going further than the Cubists, Russian painter Kasimir Malevich (1878–1935) reaches abstraction by reducing his paintings to pure arrangements of flat geometrical shapes. He calls this style suprematism.

TRANSATLANTIC SPEECH

Radio transmits speech across the Atlantic Ocean for the first time. It is sent from a U.S. naval base in Virginia and received in Paris by a station on the Eiffel Tower.

HEATPROOF GLASS

By adding boric oxide to the mix, the Corning Glass Works in New York makes the heat-resistant glass known as Pyrex™. Ideal for ovenware, the new substance is developed by technologists Eugene Sullivan and William Taylor.

PAUL EHRLICH
(1854–1915)

Chemist, bacteriologist, hematologist, German-born Paul Ehrlich has died. He pioneered the use of chemotherapy, formulated a successful treatment for syphilis, and in 1908 shared the Nobel Prize for medicine with Ilya Mechnikov for their work in immunology.

NO QUIET ON THE WESTERN FRONT

War continues to engulf the globe. As always, war stimulates technology and a new weapon appears, the tank. It is first used on the Somme. Plastic surgery, too, develops as a result of terrible injuries and the term "shell shock" comes into use. The Easter Rising in Ireland is put down brutally. Rasputin, the monk, is murdered in Russia. The art movement Dadaism appears as a protest against the carnage of war.

OPPOSITE: Tanks first come into use in World War I. They are a British invention and first see service at Cambrai in France.

1916

Jan	6	British House of Commons votes to introduce military conscription
	16	Battle of Gallipoli ends after nine months, with an Allied withdrawal
Feb	21	Battle of Verdun begins with German attack, ends Dec. 18
Apr	25	The Easter Rising in Ireland begins; it is crushed within a week
May	21	Battle of Jutland begins; it continues until June 1
June	6	Field Marshal Lord Kitchener, British War Minister, is drowned when the cruiser he was riding sank
	21	Arab leader Hussein, Sheik of Mecca, opens a rebellion against the Turks who control Arabia

July	1	First Battle of the Somme begins on the Western Front; it lasts until November 18. Losses on both sides amount to more than 1,260,000 killed or wounded
Sep	15	British first use tanks during the Battle of the Somme
Nov	11	In a close vote, Woodrow Wilson is reelected
	21	Emperor Franz Joseph of Austria-Hungary dies at the age of 86
Dec	5	David Lloyd George becomes prime minister in the U.K.
	30	Grigori Rasputin, self-styled "holy man" and adviser to the Czarina of Russia, is murdered by a group of noblemen

ABOVE: Armored cruisers, or Dreadnoughts, steaming in formation.

MEXICAN REVOLUTION

In Mexico, soldiers of the rebel leader Pancho Villa cross into the U.S.A. and kill eighteen Americans working for a mining company. In response, US troops under General Pershing march into Mexico and attack Villa, killing 30 of his men and routing his army.

EASTER RISING

Rebel Irish republicans seize strategic buildings in central Dublin on Easter Sunday and declare an Irish Republic. The British bombard the city to end the rebellion, which spreads to other cities in Ireland, and they execute the leaders. As a result, support for Irish independence increases throughout Ireland.

RASPUTIN

In Petrograd, a group of Russian nobles murder Rasputin, the Siberian monk and mystic who has held considerable power over the czar's wife and is blamed for exercising a malign control over affairs of state.

EASTER 1916

The Irish poet W.B. Yeats (1865–1939), who is already well known, writes the poem "Easter 1916" on the Dublin Easter Rising. The poem is well known for its celebration of Irish nationalist heroes and for its line "A terrible beauty is born." Later, in 1922, after the Anglo-Irish War, Yeats will become a senator in the Irish Free State.

ARAB REVOLT

Arabs rise in revolt against their Ottoman rulers in Hejaz, Saudi Arabia. The revolt is led by Emir Feisal and his son Hussein and is supported from December by Colonel T.E. Lawrence, a British soldier with close links to the Arab rebels.

BRITISH CONSCRIPTION

In the United Kingdom, the House of Commons agrees to introduce conscription to increase the size of the army. The government has been relying on single men to volunteer, but losses on the Western Front mean that volunteers can no longer be relied upon to ensure the army remains at full strength.

AUSTRO-HUNGARIAN EMPEROR DIES

Franz Josef, Emperor of Austria-Hungary, dies at the age of 86 after ruling his country since 1848. He is succeeded by his grandnephew, Charles I.

BIRTH OF THE TANK

First trials of a military tank take place in Britain. It is first used in battle on the Somme. The name "tank" is used to confuse German spies. This new weapon of war is an armored vehicle, which can cross the most difficult terrain and withstand powerful artillery.

PLASTIC SURGERY

British surgeon Harold Gillies sets up a plastic surgery unit to deal with 2,000 cases of facial damage after the Battle of the Somme.

SHELL SHOCK

This year the term "shell shock" comes into use to describe the psychological disorder caused by battle fatigue and experiences in the trenches. It is often mistakenly regarded as a form of cowardice.

SPHERES OF INFLUENCE

Leaders of Great Britain and France have reached an agreement to divide the Middle East. Both countries agree to concede the town of Constantinople and the Turkish Straits to Russia. France will control Syria, Cilia, and Adana, while Great Britain will receive Palestine and Mesopotamia.

DADAISM

In Zurich, a group of young artists found the Dada movement, an anti-art movement that has its roots in their protest against the carnage of World War I. They start the Cabaret Voltaire, where they put on bizarre lectures and weird entertainments. They revel in nonsense and the irrational and many of their number (who include Marcel Duchamp, Jean Arp, and the Romanian poet Tristan Tzara) will later become prominent Surrealists.

UNDER FIRE

French writer Henri Barbusse (1873–1935) publishes *Under Fire*. An anti-war novel, it is based on Barbusse's own experiences at the front. It portrays, unusually for these patriotic times, the squalid side of war and the lives of ordinary men in the trenches.

RELATIVITY

German theoretical physicist Albert Einstein publishes his General Theory of Relativity, which argues that the gravity of a mass, such as a heavenly body, distorts space.

DETERGENTS

German scientist Fritz Gunther develops the first synthetic detergents to replace soap. They prove to be too harsh for domestic use.

THE PLANETS

British composer Gustav Holst (1874–1934) writes this suite for large orchestras, inspired by his own studies of astrology. Despairing of the chances of such a large-scale work getting performed, he puts the score away. When friends discover the work and have it performed for Holst, the composer's handling of rhythm and orchestral color will win over both audience and musicians alike.

FIRST GUIDE DOGS

In Austria and Germany the first guide dogs for the blind are trained to help soldiers blinded in battle.

BOEING TAKES OFF

U.S. industrialist William E. Boeing (1881–1954) founds the Pacific Aero Products Company, later the Boeing Company, one of the largest aircraft manufacturers.

NO OLYMPICS

The First World War forces the cancellation of the Olympic Games.

BIRTH CONTROL CLINIC

The U.S.A.'s first birth control clinic opens in New York, run by Margaret Sanger (1883–1966), a public health nurse. Like the pioneering clinic opened in 1878 in Amsterdam, the Brooklyn clinic is technically illegal. Mrs. Sanger was jailed in 1914 for distributing birth control literature.

FIRST CONGRESSWOMAN

Jeannette Rankin (1880–1975), a worker for women's rights, becomes the first woman to be elected to the U.S. Congress. Her stance on the war in Europe is pacifist and she will fight for independent citizenship for married women.

NATIONAL PARKS

The National Parks Service is set up by the U.S. government. President Cleveland pioneered the creation of parks and preserves during the nineteenth century. Since 1872, the USA has protected over twenty areas of natural and scientific interest.

HORATIO HERBERT KITCHENER (1850–1916)

Lord Kitchener, the Irish-born British field marshal, has been lost at sea after his ship HMS *Hampshire* was mined off Orkney in June. He was veteran of the Sudan campaign (1883–1885) and commanded British forces in South Africa during the second Boer War (1900–1902) and in India (1902–1909). Appointed British secretary for war in 1914, he was responsible for a highly successful recruitment campaign.

WORLD WAR I

Sometimes called "the Great War" or "the war to end all wars," World War I is fought in Europe, Africa, the Middle and Far East. On one side are the Central European powers (Germany, Austria-Hungary and allies); on the other are the Triple Entente (Britain and Empire, France, Russia and allies) together with the United States of America, which enters the war in 1917. An estimated 10 million people die and twice that number are wounded.

❖KEY DATES❖
WESTERN FRONT 1914–1918 FRANCE AND BELGIUM

- **NAMUR August 20–25, 1914.** German heavy artillery, including 540 heavy guns, batter Belgian fort into surrender, inflicting over 30,000 casualties.
- **MONS August 23–24, 1914.** The British 2nd Corps conducts a fighting withdrawal in the face of heavy German attacks. For losses of 1,600, British marksmen inflict 3,000 casualties on the Germans.
- **FIRST BATTLE OF THE MARNE September 6–8, 1914.** The battle that saves Paris, the Germans commit 44 infantry and 7 cavalry divisions, the Allies 56 infantry and 9 cavalry divisions. German casualties are 200,000, French 250,000, and British 1,071.
- **YPRES October 14–November 11, 1914.** The German offensive. It costs Germany 130,000 casualties, the French 50,000, the British 2,368 officers and 55,768 men, and the Belgians 32,000.
- **YPRES April 22–May 25, 1915.** Germans use poison gas against the British. Its use and subsequent fighting cause 60,000 Allied casualties and 35,000 German.
- **VERDUN February 21–December 18, 1916.** A grim battle of attrition. The Germans fire 40 million shells. Initially, 1,000,000 Germans attack 500,000 French, At the close, the Germans have lost 434,000 and the French 543,000.
- **FIRST BATTLE OF THE SOMME July 1–Nov 18, 1916.** British lose 57,470 men on the first day. By November 18, the Allies have advanced 7 miles over a 20 mile front. The British lose 418,000, the French 195,000, and the Germans 650,000 (killed or wounded).
- **YPRES July 21–November 6, 1917.** A British offensive is designed in part to take the pressure off the French. Germany counterattacks and the use of bunkers causes heavy casualties of 400,000 while the Germans suffer 65,000, including 9,000 prisoners.
- **CAMBRAI November 20–December 4, 1917.** The first great tank battle in which 324 tanks are committed and make a 6 mile gap in the German lines. The Germans counterattack and when the fighting is over the British have lost 43,000 including 6,000 prisoners, the Germans 41,000 including 11,000 prisoners.

- **SECOND BATTLE OF THE SOMME March 21–April 4, 1918.** A massive assault by 71 German divisions with 6,000 guns, the Germans advance 40 miles but are halted by exhaustion and lack of supplies. The Allies lose 160,000 battle casualties and 70,000 prisoners, the Germans 150,000 killed or wounded.
- **VILLERS-BRETONNEUX April 24, 1918.** The first tank versus tank action; three British Mark IV tanks fight a drawn engagement with three German heavy A7Vs.
- **SECOND BATTLE OF THE MARNE July 15–August 6, 1918.** A major German attack by 52 divisions which is stopped by 36 Allied divisions, French, American, British and Italian. The Germans lose 100,000 and the Allies lose 60,000, including 20,000 dead.

❖KEY DATES❖
EASTERN FRONT 1914–1917 RUSSIA POLAND, AUSTRIA, HUNGARY, ROMANIA

- **TANNENBERG August 26–30,1914.** A massive German victory against the Russians. Russia loses 30,000 killed or wounded and 92,000 prisoners. The Germans lose 13,000 killed or wounded.
- **GORLICE-TARNOW April 28–August 5, 1915.** Germany and Austria advance through Poland and the Ukraine. Pounded by heavy artillery, the Russians lose one million killed or wounded and one million prisoners as well as huge areas of valuable agricultural land.
- **LAKE NAROTCH March 18, 1916.** After initial successes, the Russian infantry is counterattacked and loses more than 80,000 men.

❖ KEY DATES ❖
NAVAL WAR

- **CORONEL November 1, 1914.** Five German cruisers, the *Gneisenau*, *Scharnhorst*, *Nürnberg*, *Dresden* and *Leipzig*, meet and destroy HMS *Good Hope* and HMS *Monmouth*. The smaller and faster HMS *Glasgow* is able to escape.
- **FALKLANDS December 8, 1914.** HMS *Invincible*, *Inflexible*, *Kent*, *Cornwall*, *Glasgow*, *Bristol*, *Otranto* and *Macedonia* meet and destroy the German squadron that was victorious at the Coronel. Only *Dresden* escapes.
- **DARDANELLES February 19–March 18, 1915.** A Franco-British attempt to block the straits of the Dardanelles is unsuccessful. A combination of mines and coastal batteries sinks three heavy ships and damages three.
- **JUTLAND May 21–June 1, 1916.** Germans lose four cruisers and five destroyers. They claim victory because the British navy loses three battle cruisers, three light cruisers, and eight destroyers. British claim victory because German fleet does not venture to sea again and the Allied naval blockade of Germany remains intact.

❖ KEY DATES ❖
AIR WAR IN THE WEST 1914–1918

- **August 14, 1914.** First bombing attack of World War I, undertaken by an aircraft of French Aviation Militaire against zeppelin sheds, at Metz-Frescaty.
- **August 30, 1914.** First bombing attack on a capital city, Paris. German Taube drops five bombs and a message; one person killed, two wounded.
- **October 5, 1914.** The first aircraft is shot down in air-to-air combat.
- **April 15–26, 1916.** First aerial resupply mission, Kut-el-Amara, Mesopotamia. Food, mail, currency, gold, silver and wireless parts are delivered by the RFC and RNAS.
- **April 5–6, 1917.** First British night bombing begins, hitting aircraft hangars at Douai airfield.
- **June 13, 1917.** German Gotha bombers make first and most costly mass bombing raid on London. Fourteen Gotha bombers drop 72 bombs killing 162 and injuring 432 people.

❖ KEY DATES ❖
MEDITERRANEAN AND MIDDLE EAST 1914–1918 EGYPT, PALESTINE AND MESOPOTAMIA

- **GALLIPOLI April 25, 1915–January 16, 1916.** Amphibious landing on the Turkish coast which, through British mismanagement, fails to block the narrows of the Dardanelles. After heavy fighting, the Allies are obliged to withdraw. Allied casualties are 252,000 and Turkish casualties are 251,000, including 66,000 deaths.
- **ISONZO RIVER (Italian Front) June 23, 1915–October 1917.** Eleven battles in all. Italian troops launch attacks against Austrian positions on the Isonzo River. Four battles fought in 1915 cost the Italians 66,000 killed, 185,000 wounded, and 22,000 taken prisoner, for no real gains.
- **KUT-EL-AMARA December 8, 1915–April 29, 1916.** Initial British successes are followed by a decision to fortify and hold Kut, leading to a siege and British defeat. 10,000 starving and sick survivors surrender to the Turks.
- **CAPORETTO October 24–November 12, 1917.** Seven German and eight Austrian divisions attack General Capello's mutinous 2nd Italian army. The Italians are driven back to the Brenta valley at Caporetto and the Italians lose 40,000 killed or wounded.
- **JERUSALEM December 11, 1917.** General Allenby enters Jerusalem following the defeat of the Turks at Nebi Samwil ridge. He guarantees religious toleration to all.
- **WADI FARA September, 1918.** First major ground attack victory by a British squadron of SE5s against retreating Turkish troops.
- **VITTORIO VENETO October 24–November 4, 1918.** Italians with 57 divisions and 7,700 guns attack the Austrians with 52 divisions and 6,000 guns. Italians, with British and French assistance, force crossings over the Piave and capture Vittorio Veneto. Victory leads to the collapse of the Austro-Hungarian empire. The Austrians lose 5,000 guns and 300,000 prisoners while Italian casualties are 36,000.

WAR AND REVOLUTION

The United States enters the war on the Allied side. A revolution occurs in Russia that ends with the Bolsheviks victorious and the formation of the world's first Communist state. Its effects will be felt for most of the century. In science, a development occurs that will dominate the century: Rutherford splits the atom, paving the way for the nuclear age.

OPPOSITE TOP: Poison gas in the trenches. First used by the Germans, gas had devastating effects.

OPPOSITE BELOW: Australian troops being treated at a dressing station near Ypres.

1917

Jan	10	William F. Cody, better known as Buffalo Bill, dies
Feb	3	The United States severs diplomatic relations with Germany
Mar	8	Count Ferdinand von Zeppelin, airship designer, dies at age 78
	10	Russian workers in Petrograd demonstrate against the war and widespread famine
	14	Provisional government set up in Russia
	16	Russia's ruler Czar Nicholas II abdicates
	16-17	German U-boats sink three U.S. ships
Apr	6	United States declares war on Germany
	16	With German help, Bolshevik revolutionary Vladimir Lenin returns to Russia after ten years in exile

June	24	First American soldiers land in France
July	16	Alexander Kerensky becomes prime minister of Russia
	31	On the Western Front, the Battle of Passchendaele begins in a sea of mud. It lasts until November 10
Sep	17	Germany captures the port of Riga
Nov	2	Balfour Declaration: British Foreign Secretary Arthur Balfour promises the Jews a homeland in Palestine
	7	"October Revolution" in Russia; Lenin and Bolsheviks seize power
	17	French sculptor Auguste Rodin dies at age 77
Dec	6	Finland declares independence from Russia
	15	Russia signs an armistice with Germany

UKRAINE AND FINLAND INDEPENDENT

As a result of the Russian Revolution, Ukraine declares itself a republic and breaks away from Russia. Finland follows the next month and is recognized by the new Russian government as an independent state.

UNITED STATES ENTERS THE WAR

In April, the United States enters the war on the Allied side against Germany. President Wilson declares that "the world must be made safe for democracy." U.S. resources, including shipbuilding and steel production, are put to work for the war effort as thousands of troops prepare to sail for Europe.

WOMEN'S WAR WORK

British and French women sign up for war work in munitions factories, agriculture, transport, and the auxiliary military units from 1915, and American women after April 1917. In the United States and Britain especially, their contribution softens attitudes to women's emancipation.

JEWISH HOMELAND

Arthur Balfour, British Foreign Secretary, issues a declaration promising the Jews a homeland of their own in Palestine. The British government hopes that the declaration will lead to Jewish support for the war effort.

DE STIJL

Dutch painter, poet, and architect Theo van Doesburg (1883–1931) founds the magazine *De Stijl* (the style). The De Stijl artists, including Mondrian and Gerrit Rietveld, embrace a theory of art that can also be applied to painting, architecture, and the decorative arts. They use primary colors and right angles, and reject art that takes its inspiration from nature.

RADIOACTIVE ELEMENT FOUND

Two teams of scientists independently discover the element protactinium, a radioactive metal; they are Otto Hahn (1879–1968) and Lise Meitner (1878–1968) of Germany, and Frederick Soddy and John Cranston of Britain.

MATA HARI SHOT

Mata Hari is executed in France as a spy. She was Netherlands-born Margaretha Geertruida Zelle who, after divorcing her Scottish husband, became a dancer in Paris. In 1907 she joined the German secret service and betrayed military secrets confided by unsuspecting Allied officers.

DETERGENT

The first artificial detergent, called Nekal, is produced commercially in Germany during World War I for washing clothes, to conserve soap for other purposes. Synthetic chemical detergents wash clothes cleaner than soap.

HILAIRE GERMAIN EDGAR DEGAS (1834–1917)

Edgar Degas, the French impressionist painter and sculptor, dies at the age of 83. His paintings and pastel work portray the movement and line of horses and their riders, circus artists, and ballet dancers. Among his best-known and best-loved works are *Absinthe* (1876–1877), *Dancer Lacing her Shoe* (1878), and *Miss Lola at the Cirque Fernando* (1879).

HUGE TELESCOPE

American astronomer George E. Hale (1868–1938) installs a 3 yard refracting telescope at Mount Wilson Observatory in California, of which he is director. Hale's telescope is the world's largest to date.

SPLITTING THE ATOM

British scientist Ernest Rutherford (1871–1937) bombards nitrogen atoms and breaks up the nucleus, thus becoming the first person to split the atom. He does not publish his results until 1919, but his achievement will have enormous and long-lasting implications.

SONAR BEGINS

French physicist Paul Langevin (1872–1946) invents a method of detecting sound under water. It is later developed as sonar (an acronym of Sound Navigation And Ranging) and used for locating submarines.

FIRST AIRMAIL STAMP

Italy issues the first airmail stamp in May by overprinting a 25 centime express letter stamp with ESPERIMENTO POSTA AEREA MAGGIO 1917 TORINO-ROMA-ROMA-TORINO.

BOBBED HAIR

A short haircut known as the bob, pioneered by Irene Castle, is adopted for safety by women workers in munitions factories and becomes the latest fashion in hairstyles.

DIXIELAND JAZZ

The Original Dixieland Jazz Band makes its first recording: *The Darktown Strutters' Ball*.

NAIL VARNISH

Transparent liquid nail varnish is first manufactured by Cutex.

BRITS CAPTURE JERUSALEM

The British infantry, led by General Edmund "The Bull" Allenby, capture Jerusalem. Their victory was aided by earlier raids on transportation facilities led by T.E. Lawrence, "Lawrence of Arabia."

RUSSIAN REVOLUTION

Czar Nicholas II (1868–1918) abdicates in March as revolution breaks out across Russia. Discontent with the unpopular war against Germany and Austria, high loss of life on the Eastern Front, and food shortages at home combine to weaken the czar's authority. A provisional government is set up after the czar's brother refuses to accept the throne. In July, the Bolshevik party, led by Vladimir Ilych Lenin (1870–1924), fails to take power in Russia after an abortive coup. Lenin flees in disgrace and Alexander Kerensky (1881–1970), a socialist member of the Duma and Minister of War in the provisional government, becomes prime minister. He promises to continue the war against Germany. In November, October in the Russian calendar, the Bolsheviks overthrow the provisional government of Alexander Kerensky and seize power in a bloodless coup. The Bolsheviks promise "Peace, land, bread, and all power to the Soviets." The new government, led by Lenin, opens peace negotiations with the Germans.

ABOVE: The luxurious lifestyle of the czars clashed with the deep poverty experienced by most Russians.

ABOVE: During the Revolution of 1917 important buildings were protected from damage and looting.

ABOVE: Crowds outside the Winter Palace, St. Petersburg, scene of the revolution.

RIGHT: The ex-czar Nicholas II, in exile under guard, the last of the Russian royals this century.

PEACE COMES AND EUROPE IS REDRAWN

Germany surrenders and World War I ends. Postwar peace settlements involve the breakup of the old Austro-Hungarian empire and redraw the map of Europe. In Russia, the Romanovs are shot and civil war breaks out as the Bolsheviks fight to protect the revolution. Women in Britain gain the vote. Airmail services begin in the United States.

1918

Jan	9	U.S. President Woodrow Wilson lists 14 points for U.S. war aims
Mar	3	Russia signs Treaty of Brest-Litovsk with Germany
	21	Germans begin series of three offensives on Western Front
Apr	22	German flying ace, the "Red Baron," is shot down and killed during the Second Battle of the Somme
July	16	In Russia, Bolsheviks execute Czar Nicholas and his family
Sep	26	Final Allied offensive begins on the Western Front
Nov	4	Austria signs an armistice with the Allies
	9	After riots in Germany, Kaiser Wilhelm II abdicates and Germany becomes a republic
	11	World War I ends Austria's emperor Karl abdicates
	13	Austria and Hungary are declared republics

ABOVE: British nurses celebrate the end of the carnage.

OPPOSITE: The guns fall silent at last on the 11th hour of the 11th month, 1918.

WILSON'S 14 PEACE POINTS

In a speech to Congress, in January, U.S. President Wilson sets out 14 points for a peace settlement. Among them are the breakup of Austria-Hungary, the independence of Poland, and the establishment of an international organization to guarantee the independence and integrity of all nations.

RUSSIA OUT OF THE WAR

Germany and Russia sign a peace treaty at Brest-Litovsk in Poland, which takes Russia out of the war. Russia is forced to cede Poland and the Baltic states to Germany and large areas of the Caucasus to the Ottoman Empire, as well as recognize the independence of Ukraine. The treaty allows Germany to transfer its large armies to the Western Front.

CZAR SHOT

As Russia collapses into civil war, the former Russian czar, Nicholas II, and his family are shot by the Bolsheviks to prevent them falling into counter-revolutionary hands. The Bolsheviks organize a Red Army under Leon Trotsky (1879–1940), commissar for war, to fight for the revolution.

WAR ENDS

As Germany collapses, Kaiser Wilhelm II flees into exile in the Netherlands. On November 11, Germany and the Allies finally sign a peace treaty. The Ottoman Empire and Austria also sue for peace. After more than four years of bitter fighting, World War I comes to an end. As an approximate estimate, more than ten million people have been killed.

NEW NATIONS

Following peace settlements, four new nations emerge out of the old multinational Austro-Hungarian empire. Austria and Hungary become independent republics, as does Czechoslovakia. The South Slavs form a new kingdom, later called Yugoslavia, which is ruled by King Peter of Serbia, who led his country to victory in the war.

WINNING THE VOTE

After a 67 year struggle, women in Britain finally gain the vote. New legislation gives the vote to women over the age of 30 and men over 21.

WILFRED OWEN
(1893–1918)

The young English poet, Wilfred Owen, is killed in action just one week before the end of World War I. His friend, the poet Siegfried Sassoon, will collect his unpublished work for publication in 1920. Owen's famous poems "Dulce et Decorum Est" and "Anthem for Doomed Youth" are heartfelt appeals against war and its brutality.

ACHILLE-CLAUDE DEBUSSY
(1862–1918)

Claude Debussy has died after a long battle with cancer. The Parisian composer was responsible for the creation of musical Impressionism and has had a strong influence on contemporary composers. His works include the orchestral tone poem *Le Mer* (1905), chamber music, piano pieces, and many lovely song settings.

THE TWELVE

Set in St. Petersburg during the Bolshevik revolution, "The Twelve," a poem by Russian poet Alexander Blok, describes a group of 12 Red Guards. A tribute to the revolution that uses techniques as diverse as folk songs and revolutionary slogans, the work portrays the revolutionaries as if they were the Apostles of Christ.

CALLIGRAMMES

The second of French writer Guillaume Apollinaire's two volumes of verse, *Calligrammes*, is published. The first was *Les Alcools* in 1913. It develops the technique of making the physical shape of the poems match their content. Thus, rain is depicted in type that pours vertically down the page and typography mirrors the shapes of field guns and cathedrals.

THREE-COLOR LIGHTS

Three-color traffic lights, with a yellow phase between green and red, are introduced in England and in New York City.

SUPERHET RADIO

The superheterodyne, or "superhet," radio receiver is invented by U.S. army major and electrical engineer Edwin Armstrong (1890–1954). It makes radios easier to tune. Subsequently, all radios will work on this principle.

AUSTRALIAN RADIO LINK

Using Morse code, the first-ever radio link is made between Britain and Australia.

FOOD MIXER

The universal food mixer and beater is invented by the Universal Company of America. It consists of a bowl and two beaters powered by electricity.

SUPREMATIST COMPOSITION

With his painting *White on White*, Russian artist Malevich takes his suprematist style to its logical conclusion, painting white shapes on a white background. The work becomes the symbol of extreme modernism in painting.

RIGHT: Women take up heavy work in wartime.

ABOVE: American soldier getting ready for action. Over 116,000 U.S. troops die.

RIGHT: The Red Baron, Manfred von Richthofen, the German air ace killed in action this year.

AFTERMATH OF WAR

ABOVE: Destroyed bridge over the River Meuse at Namur, Belgium.

ABOVE: Ruined fortifications near Liège, Belgium.

ABOVE: German POWs in a French camp.

ABOVE: Paris was devastated by heavy artillery.

BELOW: Passchendaele is a barren sea of mud.

PEACE OF PARIS AND THE WEIMAR REPUBLIC

The League of Nations is set up by a world temporarily sickened by the carnage of war. The Treaty of Versailles imposes reparations on Germany. In Germany, a new constitution establishes the Weimar Republic. In Italy, Mussolini founds the Fascist party. British troops fire on Sikhs in the town of Amritsar and war breaks out between British India and Afghanistan. Aviators Alcock and Brown make the first transatlantic flight.

OPPOSITE: French tennis star Suzanne Lenglen wins the Women Singles at Wimbledon.

1919

Jan	5	Spartacist uprising begins in Berlin; it is quickly suppressed	**June**	15	Aviators Alcock and Brown complete the first nonstop flight across the Atlantic Ocean
	6	Former U.S. President Theodore Roosevelt dies at age 60		28	Peace of Paris between Germany and the Allies is signed at Versailles
	18	Peace conference begins at Versailles, near Paris			
	21	Sinn Fein MPs set up an unofficial "parliament" in Dublin	**July**	5	French tennis star Suzanne Lenglen wins the Women Singles at Wimbledon
Feb	6	Bolsheviks capture Kiev, Ukraine		13	British airship R-34 completes the first two-way Atlantic flight
	14	The League of Nations is founded		31	The Weimar Republic is founded in Germany
	14	Bolsheviks invade Estonia			
	20	Emir of Afghanistan murdered			
Mar	23	Italian journalist Benito Mussolini founds the Fascist party	**Aug**	8	Afghanistan achieves independence
			Oct	7	Dutch airline KLM is founded
Apr	15	British troops massacre 379 unarmed rioters at Amritsar, India	**Nov**	15	Red Army captures Omsk
May	3	War begins between British India and Afghanistan	**Dec**	17	French artist Pierre Auguste Renoir dies at age 78

ABOVE: Captain John Alcock (left) and Lieutenant Arthur Brown (right) after their successful transatlantic flight. Alcock describes the historic journey as "terrible."

SPARTACIST UPRISING

A Communist uprising by Spartacist revolutionaries against the new German government is crushed. Its two main leaders, Karl Liebknecht and "Red" Rosa Luxemburg, are both shot.

SINN FEIN

The 73 members of parliament elected in the British general election of December 1918 to represent Sinn Féin, a republican party, set up their own Dáil Éireann, or parliament, in Dublin. The rebel parliament forms its own government in opposition to the British.

TREATY OF VERSAILLES

In June, Germany and the Allies sign a peace treaty in the Palace of Versailles, outside Paris. The treaty has 400 clauses and strips Germany of much of its territory. Germany is forced to pay reparations to the Allies and to demilitarize the Rhineland. British prime minister David Lloyd George (1863–1945) considers the treaty too tough and predicts that it will cause another war within 25 years.

LEAGUE OF NATIONS

Allied nations meet in Paris to agree on a peace settlement in Europe and hold the first meeting of the League of Nations. President Wilson presides. The peace conference later agrees to the covenant that establishes this new international body.

FASCIST PARTY SET UP

An Italian journalist, Benito Mussolini (1883–1945), who broke with the Socialist party at the outbreak of war, forms *Fasci di Combattimento*, a nationalistic party later described as fascist.

AMRITSAR MASSACRE

British troops, led by General Dyer, open fire on unarmed demonstrators in the holy Sikh city of Amritsar. The massacre follows several days of rioting caused by a business strike against new security laws and prompts widespread protests against British rule in India.

WEIMAR REPUBLIC

A new constitution is agreed upon in the German city of Weimar, establishing a republic and an all-powerful presidency. The new constitution is opposed by the extreme left and right parties.

THIRD AFGHAN WAR

Fighting breaks out between Britain and Afghanistan as Afghanistan, under Emir Amanullah Khan, objects to British intervention in Afghan affairs. After some skirmishes between British and Afghan troops, Afghanistan's sovereignty is recognized.

REDS AND WHITES

Civil war continues in Russia between the Bolshevik Red Army and the so-called Whites, or counter-revolutionaries. After nearly two years of fighting, by November, the Red Army has taken Omsk and looks set to win the war.

SMALL-TOWN STORIES

American writer Sherwood Anderson (1876–1941) brings the lives, longings, and frustrations of small-town Americans into the public gaze with his collection of linked stories, *Winesburg, Ohio*.

J'ACCUSE

This antiwar film is the first major work by French director Abel Gance (1889–1981). It is successful and launches the director on a series of epics, perhaps the most famous of which will be *Napoléon vu par Abel Gance* (1927). Gance becomes known for his innovative use of wide and split-screen techniques.

THE CABINET OF DR. CALIGARI

Starring Conrad Veidt and Werner Krauss, *The Cabinet of Dr. Caligari* by German director Robert Wiene (1881–1938) is a remarkable example of expressionism. Narrated by a madman, the film portrays a series of murders carried out by a sleepwalker at the suggestions of a mad mountebank. Its use of projected light patterns gives the film a particular horror.

FLYING THE ATLANTIC

In May, the U.S. Navy flying boat NC-4, commanded by Lieutenant Commander A.C. Read, makes the first transatlantic flight from Rockaway, New York, to Plymouth, England. Read stops seven times, including Chatham, Mass.; Halifax, Nova Scotia; Trepassy Bay, Newfoundland; Horta, Azores; Ponta Delgarda, Azores; Lisbon, Portugal; and Ferrol del Caudillo, Spain. The flight takes 23 days. One month later, two Britons, Captain John Alcock and Lieutenant Arthur Whitten-Brown, make the first nonstop Atlantic flight in a converted Vickers Vimy bomber, from St John's, Newfoundland to Clifden, Co. Galway, Ireland. Their time is 16 hours and 12 minutes. In July, the British airship R-34 makes the first lighter-than-air crossing of the Atlantic twice. The first is from Scotland to New York, the second is from New York to Norfolk, England. The distance totals 6,316 miles and the time for this first-ever double crossing is 183 hours and 8 minutes.

FIRST WOMAN MP

The first woman to take her seat in the British House of Commons is American-born Nancy Astor. She is sister of the ideal American woman, the Gibson Girl, and now MP for the Plymouth constituency.

LITTERATURE

The French writer André Breton (1896–1966), with Louis Aragon and Phillippe Soupault, founds the influential magazine, *Littérature*. It will become an organ of the surrealist movement, publishing the first example of "automatic writing" in 1920.

KLM FOUNDED

The Royal Dutch Airline, KLM, is founded in October.

PIERRE AUGUSTE RENOIR (1841–1919)

The French impressionist painter Pierre Auguste Renoir, who pioneered painting outdoors to capture the effects of light, has died. His impressionist works *Moulin de la Galette* (1876) and *The Umbrellas* (1883) are typical of his style from 1874–1884, although in later years his work becomes more formal.

ABOVE: The Vickers Vimy plane, which had carried Alcock and Brown safely across the Atlantic, grounded in a bog in Ireland.

TENNIS FASHION

Frenchwoman Suzanne Lenglen (1899–1938) ushers in a new era for women's tennis with the first of her six Wimbledon singles titles. The "Empress of the Courts" wears loose one-piece dresses when heavy outfits with collars and cuffs and petticoats were the normal attire.

CURE FOR SLEEPING SICKNESS

American scientist Louise Pearce discovers tryparsamide, a compound that cures sleeping sickness.

WEBER DISAGREES WITH MARX

Max Weber (1864–1920), German social scientist and author of *The Protestant Ethic* and the *Spirit of Capitalism*, becomes professor of sociology at Munich University. He supports a scientific approach to social science, but disagrees with Marx that economics alone determines social action. He emphasizes the effects of cultural factors, such as religion, on economic development.

PROTO-RADAR

British physicist Robert Watson-Watt (1892–1973) patents his "radiolocator," a device for locating aircraft or ships. Later it develops into radar.

POETIC JUSTICE

Italian poet and airman Gabriele D'Annunzio (1863–1938) seizes the small city of Fiume (modern Trieste) in Dalmatia on behalf of Italy. Supported by a force of 300 volunteers, he drives out the Allied government representatives and sets himself up as a dictator.

WINNERS AND ACHIEVERS OF THE 1910s

NOBEL PRIZES

The Nobel Prizes are an international award granted in the fields of literature, physics, chemistry, physiology or medicine, and peace. The first prizes were awarded in 1901 and funded by the money left in the will of the Swedish inventor, Alfred Nobel (1833–1896), who gave the world dynamite.

PRIZES FOR LITERATURE

1910 Paul von Heyse (German) for poetry, fiction and drama
1911 Maurice Maeterlinck (Belgian) for drama
1912 Gerhart Hauptmann (German) for drama
1913 Rabindranath Tagore (Indian) for poetry
1914 *No award*
1915 Romain Rolland (French) for fiction
1916 Verner von Heidenstam (Swedish) for poetry
1917 Karl Gjellerup (Danish) for poetry and fiction, and Henrik Pontoppidan (Danish) for fiction
1918 *No award*
1919 Carl Spitteler (Swiss) for fiction

PRIZES FOR PEACE

1910 The International Peace Bureau for promoting international arbitration and organizing peace conferences
1911 Tobias Asser (Dutch) for organizing conferences on international law, and Alfred Fried (Austrian) for his writings on peace as editor of *Die Friedenswarte*
1912 Elihu Root (American) for settling the problem of Japanese immigration to California and organizing the Central American Peace Conference
1913 Henri Lafontaine (Belgian) for work as president of the International Peace Bureau
1914 *No award*
1915 *No award*
1916 *No award*
1917 The International Red Cross for doing relief work during World War I
1918 *No award*
1919 Woodrow Wilson (American) for attempting a just settlement of World War I and advocating the League of Nations. (Award delayed until 1920.)

PRIZES FOR PHYSICS

1910 Johannes van der Waals (Dutch) for studying the relationships of liquids and gases
1911 Wilhelm Wien (German) for discoveries on the heat radiated by black objects
1912 Nils Dalen (Swedish) for inventing automatic gas regulators for lighthouses
1913 Heike Kamerlingh Onnes (Dutch) for experimenting with low temperatures and liquifying helium
1914 Max von Laue (German) for using crystals to measure X- rays
1915 Sir William Henry Bragg and Sir William Lawrence Bragg (British) for using X-rays to study crystal structure
1916 *No award*
1917 Charles Barkla (British) for studying the diffusion of light and the radiation of X-rays from elements
1918 Max Planck (German) for stating the quantum theory of light
1919 Johannes Stark (German) for discovering the Stark effect of spectra in electrical fields

PRIZES FOR CHEMISTRY

1910 Otto Wallach (German) for work in the field of alicyclic substances.
1911 Marie Curie (French) for the discovery of radium and polonium and for work in isolating radium and studying the compounds of radium
1912 François Grignard (French) for discovering the Grignard reagent to synthesize organic compounds, and Paul Sabatier (French) for the method of using nickel as a hydrogenation catalyst
1913 Alfred Werner (Swiss) for the coordination theory on the arrangement of atoms
1914 Theodore Richards (American) for determining the atomic weights of many elements
1915 Richard Willstatter (German) for research on chlorophyll and other coloring matter in plants
1916 *No award*
1917 *No award*
1918 Fritz Haber (German) for the Haber-Bosch process of synthesizing ammonia from nitrogen and hydrogen
1919 *No award*

PRIZES FOR PHYSIOLOGY OR MEDICINE

1910 Albrecht Kossel (German) for studying cell chemistry, proteins and nucleic substances
1911 Allvar Gullstrand (Swedish) for work on dioptrics, the refraction of light through the eye
1912 Alexis Carrel (French) for suturing blood vessels and grafting organs
1913 Charles Robert Richet (French) for studying allergies caused by foreign substances, as in hay fever
1914 Robert Barany (Austrian) for work on function and diseases of equilibrium organs in the inner ear
1915 *No award*
1916 *No award*
1917 *No award*
1918 *No award*
1919 Jules Bordet (Belgian) for discoveries on immunity

U.S. PRESIDENTS

1909–1913 President William Howard Taft, *Republican*
1909–1912 Vice President James S. Sherman
1913–1921 President Woodrow Wilson, *Democrat*
1913–1921 Vice President Thomas R. Marshall

SITES OF THE OLYMPIC GAMES

1912 SUMMER Stockholm, Sweden
WINTER *Not yet held*
1916 SUMMER *Not held*
WINTER *Not yet held*

INDIANAPOLIS 500

1910 *Not yet held*
1911 Ray Harroun
1912 Joe Dawson
1913 Jules Goux
1914 Rene Thomas
1915 Ralph DePalma
1916 Dario Resta
1917 *Not held*
1918 *Not held*
1919 Howdy Wilcox

KENTUCKY DERBY

1910 Donau
1911 Meridian
1912 Worth
1913 Donerail
1914 Old Rosebud
1915 Regret
1916 George Smith
1917 Omar Khayyam
1918 Exterminator
1919 Sir Barton

WIMBLEDON CHAMPIONS

1910 MEN Anthony F. Wilding
WOMEN Dorothea Douglass Lambert Chambers
1911 MEN Anthony F. Wilding
WOMEN Dorothea Douglass Lambert Chambers
1912 MEN Anthony F. Wilding
WOMEN Ethel Larcombe
1913 MEN Anthony F. Wilding
WOMEN Dorothea Douglass Lambert Chambers
1914 MEN Norman E. Brookes
WOMEN Dorothea Douglass Lambert Chambers
1915 *Not played*
1916 *Not played*
1917 *Not played*
1918 *Not played*
1919 MEN Gerald L. Patterson
WOMEN Suzanne Lenglen

WORLD SERIES CHAMPIONS

1910 Philadelphia Athletics defeat Chicago Cubs
1911 Philadelphia Athletics defeat New York Giants
1912 Boston Red Sox defeat New York Giants
1913 Philadelphia Athletics defeat New York Giants
1914 Boston Braves defeat Philadelphia Athletics
1915 Boston Red Sox defeat Philadelphia Athletics
1916 Boston Red Sox defeat Brooklyn Robins
1917 Chicago White Sox defeat New York Giants
1918 Boston Red Sox defeat Chicago Cubs
1919 Cincinnati Reds defeat Chicago White Sox